CODEPENDENCY IN MEN

Fix your Relationship with the Essential Recovery Plan to Overcome Codependency. Avoid the Codependency Quagmire

James Hibner

Page Intentionally left blank

Table of Contents

Introduction

In a healthy relationship, it is customary to rely on your partner for emotional support and view your partner as a teammate who helps you make decisions and navigate life's challenges.

On the other hand, in codependent relationships, reliance on a partner cross into unhealthy territory.

In this book, you will learn about what is codependency, including what causes it, signs of codependency, and how to treat it and many more.

In codependent relationships, one partner relies on the other to meet all of their needs, and the partner, in turn, requires the validation of being needed.

In simpler terms, the codependent personality is a "giver" who is always willing to sacrifice for their partner. And the other member of the relationship is a "taker" who relishes being all-important to that person.

Codependent behavior validates the person who is the "giver" and provides them with a sense of purpose.

Without having their partner rely upon them, the codependent personality might feel worthless.

Anyone who asks the question, "What is codependency?", may also wonder, "Is codependency a mental illness?"

The answer is, while codependent behavior can negatively affect a person's mental health, codependency in and of itself is not a mental illness. It is not an official diagnosis included in the Diagnostic and Statistical Manual of Mental Disorders. People may use the term "codependent personality disorder," but this is not an accurate mental health diagnosis.

That being said, codependency was initially identified in the 1940s in the context of behaviors seen among wives of men who abused alcohol.

Wives were identified as codependent. In the 1960s, Alcoholics Anonymous (AA) groups began to label loved ones of alcoholics as codependent, arguing that they, too, had an illness because they enabled the addict.

In general, the codependent personality lacks self-identity and therefore focuses on others, sacrificing themselves to meet their every need. In the context of addiction, the codependent spouse, parent, or child may focus all of their time and energy on "fixing" the addict while ignoring their own psychological needs.

In a romantic relationship, the codependent partner pleases their significant other while sacrificing their own needs and desires within the relationship.

A recent study with people demonstrating codependent behavior found that these individuals did not have a clear sense of self. They felt the need to change themselves to fit in with others, and they tended to be passive within their close relationships.

Some individuals in the study reported feeling as if they were trapped in their relationships, and they could not differentiate themselves from their partners.

These findings are in line with what is typically associated with the codependent personality: finding validation through approval from others, self-sacrificing to meet the needs of others, and finding identity and fulfillment through other people, instead of through a consistent sense of self.

Read on!

CHAPTER 1

Codependency: The Meaning and Facts

Codependency involves sacrificing one's personal needs to try to meet the needs of others. Someone who is codependent has an extreme focus outside themselves. Their thoughts and actions revolve around other people, such as spouses or relatives.

Codependency often appears in relationships which are unbalanced and unhealthy. A person with codependency often tries to save others from themselves. They may get hurt trying to "cure" a partner's addictions or abusive behaviors.

Codependency does not qualify as a mental health diagnosis, mostly because the symptoms are so widely applicable. Yet it can still cause severe distress.

Codependency may lead a person to develop other mental health concerns such as anxiety. A therapist can help a person reduce codependent behaviors and develop healthier relationships.

What It Looks Like

In psychology, codependency describes one person's behaviors and attitudes rather than the relationship as a whole. Someone who is codependent often builds their identity around helping others. They may "depend" on others to validate their self-worth. A codependent person may deny their own desires or emotions to get this approval.

Common symptoms of codependency include:

- **Low Self-Esteem:** Codependency may cause feelings of shame and worthlessness. A person may believe they do not deserve happiness. If a person does not value themselves, they may try to get others to value them. The sense of "being needed" can prompt internal gratification, even if the recipient of care does not show gratitude.

- **Poor Boundaries**: Codependent people often feel responsible for others' happiness. They can have a hard time saying "no" or putting their own needs first. They may hide their true thoughts and feelings to avoid upsetting others.

- **A Need to "Save" Others:** Codependent people may feel it is their duty to protect their loved ones from all harm. If a loved one does something wrong, they will likely try to fix the situation on loved one's behalf. Such behavior can prevent others from becoming independent or learning from their mistakes. It may also enable abuse or addiction to persist unchallenged.

- **Self-Denial:** A codependent person often prioritizes others' well-being over their own. They may deny their own needs for rest, emotional support, and self-care. They may feel guilt or anxiety when asserting their own desires. Codependent people can feel uneasy when others offer support.

- **Perfectionism:** Codependent people often project an image of self-reliance and competence. It is common for people to take on more responsibilities than they can handle. When they make an error or receive criticism, they may grow insecure.

- **Control Issues:** A codependent person may link their own self-worth to others' well-being. If a loved one fails, a codependent person may feel as if they failed themselves. Their attempts to make others' lives better may shift into controlling or possessive behavior.

Not every codependent person will show all these symptoms. But if a person shows many of these traits, they may be codependent.

Causes of Codependency

Codependency is usually rooted in childhood. Often, a child grows up in a home where their emotions are ignored or punished. This emotional neglect can give the child low self-esteem and shame. They may believe their needs are not worth attending to.

Typically, one or more parents are not filling their role as guardians. Their dysfunction could be due to addiction, mental health diagnoses, or other concerns. The child may need to perform tasks that exceed their developmental ability. For example, if a parent is regularly too drunk to fix dinner, a young child may learn to cook so the family doesn't go hungry.

Often the line between child and adult becomes blurred. If a parent isn't filling their role, a child may become a pseudo-parent for their siblings. They might change a brother's diapers or help a sister finish her homework.

Sometimes the child is expected to care for their own parent. A parent experiencing domestic violence may turn to the child as a confidante. A parent with narcissism may demand the child provide them praise and comfort. These interactions are often called *enmeshment.*

Since children are not fully grown, filling the role of "adult" can take all their effort. A child may be so focused on keeping the household running that they ignore their own needs. They may associate the caregiving role with feelings of stability and control.

As a child, codependent behaviors can be necessary for survival. In adulthood, the behaviors are not as adaptive. In fact, codependency can prevent a person from developing truly stable relationships.

Codependency and Addiction

Codependency may arise when someone is in a relationship with a person who has an addiction. The partner may abuse substances, or they may have an addiction to gambling or shopping.

The person with codependency may take on a "caretaker" role for their partner. The partner may rely on the caretaker to handle finances or household chores. If the addiction causes issues outside the relationship, the caretaker may cover for their partner. For example, someone who abuses alcohol may skip work. A codependent person may call the partner's boss on their behalf and claim their partner is ill.

The caretaker often cares for their partner out of a sincere desire to help. Yet their behavior often enables their partner to continue the addiction. When the caretaker "saves" the partner from consequences, the partner often loses motivation to change. They may not seek the professional rehab they need. Without help, the addiction may get worse.

That said, the caretaker is not to blame for the other person's addiction. While codependency can contribute to someone refusing treatment, it is not the only cause. Barring a safety crisis, someone cannot force others into rehabilitation.

This relationship can also harm the caretaker. The codependent person often throws their own needs to the side to care for the partner. Their codependent habits can worsen with time. They are unlikely to seek treatment for their own mental health concerns.

Codependency and Abuse

Codependency can also develop from living in an abusive household or relationship. Emotional abuse can make people feel small or unimportant. Codependent behaviors can develop as a way to counteract those feelings.

For example, someone may act as caretaker for a person with addiction in order to feel needed. Another individual may try to earn gratitude by catering to others' needs at a cost to themselves. "Saving" others can make people feel empowered and important.

A person with codependency may feel responsible for the abusive individual. If an abuser has an untreated mental health concern, the person may try to "heal" them with care. Yet love alone is not enough to treat a mental health condition. The abusive person will need professional care to begin recovery.

Some people in codependent households may feel like they are protecting their family by keeping their problems private. But enabling one party's abuse often causes harm to the other family members. Failing to report child abuse can make a person an "accessory after the fact," and bring about legal consequences.

Codependency and Parenting

Parents with codependency may try to live vicariously through their children. Some parents may try to protect a child from all hardship in life. Others may try to control a child so they grow up to meet the parent's definition of success.

This behavior can increase the risk of codependency in children. When children are allowed to explore the world and make their own plans, they develop a sense of independence. When parents make all the decisions, children may learn to ignore their own desires. They can also learn to place others' approval above their own needs.

These effects can last for years. A codependent child may lack confidence and struggle to make decisions as an adult. They may seek out relationships in which someone else has all the power. Without help, the cycle of codependency may continue for another generation.

Codependency and Caregiving

Caregivers spend their days caring for a loved one who has a chronic illness or disability. They may provide transportation, help the person bathe, or offer other day-to-day assistance. Caregiving is often difficult in and of itself. Yet codependency can further complicate the dynamic.

If you are a caregiver, you may wonder about your own behavior. Where do you draw the line between typical caregiving and codependency? Every situation is different, but if you display the following signs, there may be cause for concern:

- Insisting a loved one do everything your way. When there is an issue of safety or health, you may need to put your foot down. But it is not necessary to make every decision for the person. If your loved one wishes to wear a certain shirt, you do not need to steer them toward a more fashionable wardrobe.

- Revolving your entire life around the loved one. Caregiving can take up a lot of time and energy. Yet it is important to rest on occasion and to have a social life outside of your loved one. Otherwise you may grow resentful and burnt out.

- Encouraging your loved one to rely on you alone. Many people like to feel needed. Yet if you see other caregivers as "rivals" or discourage your loved one from being self-sufficient, there may be an issue.

- Codependency can cause a lot of strain between you and your loved one. Addressing codependent behaviors may improve your relationship. Setting boundaries and practicing communication can make a stressful situation a little healthier.

Co-Occurring Mental Health Conditions

Although codependency is not a diagnosis, it can interfere with a person's well-being. People with codependency are more likely to have low self-esteem and strong feelings of shame. Research has found relationships between codependency and the following conditions:

- Depression

- Anxiety

- Borderline personality

- Dependent personality

- Eating and food issues

Codependency is also a risk factor for substance addiction. Addiction can develop as a way to avoid difficult emotions. Some people may abuse substances to bond with a partner who is also addicted. A partner may also pressure the person with codependency into using drugs or alcohol.

If you think you may be codependent, you might wish to find a therapist. A mental health professional can determine if your behaviors resemble codependency. They can also treat any co-occurring mental health issues. In therapy, you can explore the roots of your behavior and learn to balance your needs with those of others.

CHAPTER 2

Codependency and Friendships

In recent years, we've seen a surge in mental health awareness. People has opened up about their struggles with anxiety and depression. Whether the discussion surrounds depression, anxiety, breaking generational trauma, or–one of my personal favorites–undoing conditioning, people are realizing we don't have to tackle our struggles alone.

Why do some of us rely on our friends to fulfill all of our emotional needs? There was certainly something there to unpack, as this seemed to be a recurring theme across my friendships. Could this entire dynamic be rooted in codependency?

Codependency has become a buzzword, but it is important to know that it is not classified as an official disorder or mental illness by the standards of the American Psychiatric Association's Diagnostics manual. It is, however, something we all should take seriously as it can be at the root of toxic relationships. According to the American Psychological Association, codependency is defined as an unhealthy devotion to a relationship at the cost of one's personal and psychological needs. In a study performed by the association, it was found to be correlated with greater self-consciousness, social anxiety, and dysfunctional attachment styles.

Like all of the other behavioral patterns we exhibit, codependency is usually learned through our family dynamics.

Signs of a Codependent Friendship

Consciously or unconsciously, one person in the friendship typically assumes the role of "giver" by offering the majority of the emotional, physical, or mental support. This other friend unintentionally becomes the "taker." This kind of friendship can seem harmless in the beginning. The problem arises when the taker–who is most in need of support–is unable to give the same in return.

Eventually, with the relationship being defined by an imbalance of power that leans towards the taker's needs, this leaves the perpetual giver depleted. Kim L. Knight, New York-based LMHC featured on Therapy For Black Girls, expounds on this. She says, "when there is an imbalance in the friendship, one might find themselves feeling drained or overwhelmed when talking or being around the friend. This is also a sign that codependency is at play."

She continued: "codependent friendships are often not created intentionally. They often form out of both people getting their needs fulfilled in an unhealthy manner. One person who 'needs' (the taker) and another who 'needs to be needed' (the giver). The needs for each person set the stage for an unhealthy, imbalanced relationship that leads to burn out, anger, resentment, and overall codependency."

Like all of the other behavioral patterns we exhibit, codependency is usually learned through our family dynamics. When discussing codependency on the Therapy for Black Girls podcast, licensed therapist Nedra Glover Tawwab says, "lots of times codependency looks like people who don't have healthy boundaries. Sometimes, we can see this when we have parents who may nurture us to be a certain sort of person, so you don't have the opportunity to develop boundaries," she continued.

Knight added, "lack of boundaries in friendships can also lead to codependency because there is no sense of where one person ends and the other one begins." Additionally, she goes on to note that the expectation is set and the demands are high where one person is in constant need of being "rescued," leaving the other person feeling responsible for saving them. Through this dynamic, the self- assumed giver makes it easy for the taker to avoid responsibility, and the hard work required to make a personal change. A codependent friendship can also look like:

- Relying on one friend for all of your needs and making them feel responsible for all your feelings, thoughts, actions, choices, or overall well-being.

- Giving up other friendships, hobbies, interests, or family-time to spend time with your friend.

- A fear of abandonment that can show up as feelings of jealousy if your friend spends time with other friends.

- Doing things you don't really want to do and feeling resentful about it later on.

- Feeling anxious or stressed out if you don't talk to your friend for a day or don't know what's going on with them.

- Trying to fix, control, or save your friend.

- Your self-worth and identity are dependent on your ability to care for your friend or how they are functioning.

Knight says, "relationships that are balanced have an even exchange of giving and taking. When one person starts to ignore their own needs for the sake of another on a regular basis, you are more than likely in a codependent relationship."

Noticing some of these signs in your friendships? Transformation is possible.

Noticing codependency in your friendships doesn't automatically mean that the relationship is unhealthy; it's the frequency and intensity in which they arise. One person should not feel like they are constantly giving while receiving little or nothing in return. If you can identify with this sort of friendship dynamic, there are steps you can take to achieve a healthier and interdependent friendship. Tawwab says, "the cure to codependency is healthy boundaries and committing to creating a version of yourself that is separate from others. Codependency is an unhealthy cycle of behaviors that you exhibit in relationships. You can break the cycle."

Tawwab also notes that the first thing to assess is whether or not you have any boundaries. You should feel unrestricted in letting your friend know what you will and won't do. For example, if you have a limit on how much quality time you can spend with them but they insist on seeing you every other day, make it clear that you need alone time to recharge. These are some other steps to take:

- Be honest with your friend about what you've been feeling.
- Realize that no one person can meet all your needs. It's important to spend time with other friends or family.
- Prioritize self-care. Do things that bring you joy, make you feel fulfilled, and support a healthy lifestyle.
- Be firm, but not aggressive, with your friend about what you need emotionally or mentally. They can't know what you need through passive-aggressive behavior. Tell them directly. Counseling and self-help materials may also help you better understand the root of your codependent behaviors.

CHAPTER 3

Dangers of Being in a Codependent Relationship

Codependency in relationships can be extremely toxic, especially to the individual who is struggling with the codependent issues. A codependent person tends to make their relationship more important than anything else—including their own well-being. Those on whom the individual is codependent often give very little of themselves, continuing the cycle of codependent behavior. This type of codependency can be extremely harmful to both parties, often more dangerous for the individual struggling with the codependency issues.

Meaning of Codependency

Many people have heard of codependency and understand that it can be harmful in a relationship. But, what does being codependent mean? Some people interpret codependency as an extreme dependence on someone else, a strong need for the companionship of another. Although this might be part of it, this is not the entire definition of codependency.

Codependency is a mental and emotional problem that affects the way people interact and connect with others in an interpersonal relationship. It creates problems in relationships as it causes people to become uncomfortable with themselves. Many codependent people have low self-esteem and struggle to think well of themselves. As a result, they often enter into destructive relationships that are abusive or otherwise unfulfilling.

To be codependent is to rely heavily on someone else. Often, people who are in a codependent relationships rely on a partner who actually has an addiction problem. Codependent individuals often have excessive emotional or psychological dependence on their significant other making for a relationship dynamic that is toxic and unfulfilling.

Symptoms of Codependency

There are a few key signs of codependency in a relationship that can become negative for a codependent individual. Some of the main symptoms of codependency are:

Fear of true expression: A codependent individual is less likely to voice his or her true feelings for fear of upsetting and/or scaring away his or her significant other. This can cause individuals to bottle up their emotions to the point where they develop serious health problems such as anxiety, depression, or more.

Neglecting personal needs: One of the most common traits of codependency is caring for others while neglecting personal needs. This can include going to extremes to ensure that a significant other is happy, oftentimes at the expense of the codependent individual's own well-being.

Inability to be alone: Codependency causes people to be unable to be by themselves, as they have a consistent underlying need to care for another being. Being in a relationship also helps individuals to obtain their self-esteem through others. This can lead individuals to develop an unhealthy relationship with the wrong kind of people, causing them to suffer from further emotional distress or harm.

Refusing help from others: It is typical for a codependent individual to become excessively uncomfortable when others attempt to do things for him or her. Because they associate themselves with being the caregiver or helper, individuals may find discomfort in others trying to help them, especially for fear that others will grow resentful for being put out to do so.

Being codependent and suffering from codependent relationship symptoms can cause an individual to experience numerous troubles in any (if not all) of their relationships. For example, if a codependent individual gives so much to another person and that person does not return the same sentiment, it can cause the codependent individual to grow extremely upset to the point where he or she becomes seriously depressed and other mental health issues can form thereafter.

This type of behavior can also cause an individual to enter into a relationship with someone who is likely to hurt them, as well as cause him or her to lose track of his or her own basic needs. The best way to prevent codependent behavior is to get the proper treatment to develop coping skills strong enough to negate codependency tendencies, all while promoting positive, healthy behaviors that encourage successful relationships.

There are additional symptoms of codependency that fall outside of these four codependent patterns. Many of us may even find that we have a few codependent behaviors. Because codependency is usually rooted in a person from an early age, treatment often involves exploration into early childhood issues and the correlation to current destructive behavior patterns.

Treatment involves education, experiential groups, and individual and group therapy where codependents rediscover themselves and identify self-defeating behavior patterns. Codependency is so damaging because it doesn't allow healthy relationships to flourish.

In order for people to truly give of themselves, their needs must be met as well, which means breaking codependent behaviors.

Sometimes, people who are in codependent relationships suffer from alcoholism and drug abuse. They may do so as a result of the depression and stress they experience because of their unhealthy relationships. Or, their significant other may abuse drugs and alcohol, encouraging the individual to do so, as well. This unhealthy behavior becomes learned behavior when a codependent person is acting as a negative influence.

One of the most important things a person can do in order to end codependency is to enter treatment for addiction. Through a professional rehab program, individuals can end the destructive behaviors that have been a part of their lives for so long.

The following steps can help eliminate codependency:

- **Sobriety:** Abstinence or sobriety is necessary to recover from codependency. The objective is to take your needs and wants back to yourself – to have an interior as opposed to outside "locus of control." This simply means that your actions are motivated by your values, needs and feelings, not someone else's.

- **Awareness:** Codependents tend to deny their own addiction – they deny their feelings and needs, and are not aware of why is codependency bad. This ends up leading to low self-esteem. To reverse this destructive habit, one must first become aware of them.

- **Acceptance:** Self-acceptance is an important factor in healing. Before you can change, you have to become aware of and accept the situation. In recovery, you uncover more about yourself, which requires acknowledgment. Life itself presents confinements and misfortunes to acknowledge: this is development. Welcoming reality opens the doors to possibilities, and at this point, change begins to occur.

CHAPTER 4

Gain Full Understanding of Codependency

Codependency means much more than "clinginess." Some regard codependency as a disorder or a disease, an ailment of the mind, body, and spirit, much like an addiction. For people who are living with codependency, the addiction is primarily to people and relationships with people. However, the way that their codependency manifests can be extremely different.

Codependency is a set of behaviors that cause an unhealthy attachment between one person, a codependent, and someone with whom they have become codependent. Rather than be independent or even interdependent, someone who is struggling with codependency needs to depend on someone else to create their sense of self.

Codependent relationships:

- Can be between friends, romantic partners, or family members
- Can include emotional or physical abuse
- May be recognized as such by friends and family of the codependent person
- May require the time and effort for treatment to be effective as with any mental or emotional health issue.

Through a series of thought processes, feelings, and behaviors, people who are codependent lose themselves in relationships with others and struggle to care for or be themselves. Unfortunately, this can often mean staying in abusive relationships. In the context of substance use, codependency can mean one person abuses a substance and depends on the other person to supply money, food, or shelter.

In essence, codependency means a relationship where the two people become so invested in one another that they fail to function independently. Their mood, happiness, and identity are defined by the other person.

Oftentimes there is one person in the relationship who is more passive and cannot make decisions on their own, and a more dominant person who gains some type of reward or satisfaction from controlling the other person and making their decisions.

A common sign of an unhealthy codependent relationship is the presence of enabling—a behavior used to ease tension in the relationship caused by one partner's problematic lifestyle such as continually giving them another chance, ignoring the problem, accepting excuses, or constantly coming to the rescue. There signs are generally absent in healthy relationships.

Where Does Codependency Come From?

Our codependent behaviors are modeled for us from someone else, in a variety of capacities. Typically, a primary person in our life who we have had a close relationship with has codependent behaviors with us, teaching us that this is the way love is supposed to look.

Oftentimes, codependency is born out of a household where abuse, neglect, addiction, or alcoholism play a primary role in family dynamics. In an effort to be seen, be heard, be loved, be noticed, feel important, or try to navigate the pain of abuse, we develop codependent behaviors.

Those codependent relationships can in some cases stem from childhood if there were problems with a parent where they were taught their own needs were less important than their parents' needs. Children in these situations can be taught to focus on the parent's needs rather than ever thinking of themselves. Parents who are needy may impart to their children that they are being selfish or greedy if they want anything for themselves.

We caretake, we people-please, and we put our needs beneath someone else's, all the while losing our sense of self-worth, as well as the foundation of our identity.

Why We Can't Stop Codependent Behaviors

If our codependent behaviors cause us pain and turmoil or contribute to problematic relationships, shouldn't we be able to identify these issues and remedy them?

The way we learn how to be in a relationship with ourselves and others is the way we are taught is 'normal'. We don't know any other way to be in a healthy relationship. Moreover, we often don't understand that we deserve different treatment. As the saying goes, we accept the love we believe we deserve.

Without believing we are worth a different kind of love or relationship, or knowing any other kind, we don't have the awareness that our dynamics need to change.

Common Codependent Behaviors

How codependency manifests will look different for each of us depending on our personality and our personal experiences, as well as our personal relationships.

Common codependent behaviors can include:

- Manipulation

- Emotional bullying
- Caretaking to the detriment of our own wellness
- Caregiving
- Suffocating
- People-pleasing (ignoring your own needs, then getting frustrated or angry)
- Obsession with a partner
- Excusing bad or abusive behavior
- Feeling like you need to change but can't
- Not knowing who you are without them
- Having a hard time setting boundaries
- Spending all of your time with or focused on them
- An overwhelming fear of being abandoned
- Being unable to think about life without the other person
- Being unable to believe or accept that someone loves you
- Having your partner or one person as your only close relationship
- A need for constant assurance
- Making excuses for each other

- Giving up what matters to you or makes you happy
- An inability to remember how to be alone
- Tolerating harmful behavior

Change your Life

Though it can feel as if there is no answer for codependency, there are solutions. Many books have been written about codependency, offering intimate insights into personal lives, stories of struggles, and stories of recovery.

Understanding the subconscious motivations behind partners in a codependent relationship is the key to remedying the situation. When the meaning and purpose of our life is dependent upon the existence of another person, the answer for our recovery is to place the meaning and purpose of our lives in the appropriate place. For many, this can mean having faith, believing in a Higher Power, or finding a new sense of direction and meaning. Changing codependent behaviors changes the way we live our lives, how we relate to others, and most importantly, how we relate to ourselves.

First, we get to know ourselves by taking a look at our needs, wants, and desires. Developing a basic understanding of who we are as individuals enables us to take action to nurture these small parts of ourselves through boundaries. Healthy boundaries are the firm lines we draw between ourselves and others, demonstrating what we are and what we are not willing to tolerate.

Self-care for Fixing Codependency

Outside of our relationship with others, we can foster a relationship with ourselves through self-care. This can look like many things, including the following:

Reconnecting with friends and family: codependency can mean isolating yourself, fueling the loss of self. Get in touch with those people you've distanced yourself from and begin to rebuild those relationships.

Make time for yourself: get back to those things you once enjoyed doing before you became entangled in the other person's life.

Pursue counseling: a mental health provider can help you find your sense of self and understand why you came to rely so much on the other person. Therapy can help you learn to build personal boundaries which is key to avoiding codependent relationships. Couples counseling may even be able to help or save the relationship by reducing the level of codependency.

Find substance use disorder treatment: talk to a reputable healthcare institution about your treatment options.

Some describe the journey of self-care in codependency recovery like tending to a toddler. Thinking about how we have allowed ourselves to be treated or how we have treated others, we think about whether or not we would allow such treatment toward a young child. Most often, the answer is a resounding "No!"

Thus, we embark on a journey of re-parenting the young child within us and showing ourselves all of the "perfect" love we have been missing in our lives.

CHAPTER 5

Forms of Codependency

While codependency began within the context of addiction treatment, there are multiple forms of codependencies beyond the one seen between a person with an addiction and their loved ones.

For example, codependency and relationships can take on the following forms:

- Between a parent and their children, even if the child is an adult
- Between a boyfriend and a girlfriend
- Between spouses
- Between a coworker and a boss
- Between family members, such as a grandparent and grandchild, or brother and sister

- Between friends

Codependency has the potential to derail your individuality and be exhausting for the partner that is completely focused on another. There are several causes of codependency that lead a person into an unhealthy relationship dynamic. Here are three prominent ones:

1. Alcoholism

Remember that codependent behavior was initially identified among wives of alcoholics, and there is some evidence that codependency and alcoholism are related. One study found that women who experienced symptoms of codependency with alcoholism were more likely to have a family history of alcoholism.

In such cases the codependent person can often become an enabler for the alcholic partner. The alcoholic partner might find it difficult to function normally and their partner might keep helping them perform daily tasks.

2. Dysfunctional family

Families in which children are taught to repress their emotions can cause codependency. Dysfunctional family patterns can lead people to place their feelings aside to meet the needs of others.

A dysfunctional family may also ignore problems within the family and discourage children from talking about issues. This leads people to refrain from talking or comforting each other, ultimately creating codependent adults.

3. Mental illness

Codependency can also result from growing up in a family where a parent has a severe physical or mental illness.

If all the attention is focused on meeting the needs of the sick family member, a child's needs may be set aside, creating an adult who feels guilty expressing their own needs.

Signs of Codependency

If you know what codependency is but you're wondering how to know if you're codependent, consider the following 10 signs:

- You feel responsible for other people's actions.
- You always do more than your share of the work in a relationship.
- You rely on approval and recognition from others to maintain your self-esteem.
- You feel guilty when standing up for your own needs.
- You tend to fall in love with people who you feel need "rescuing."
- You find yourself walking on eggshells to avoid conflict with your partner or with significant people in your life.
- You are the first to apologize for conflicts in your relationship, even when you haven't done anything wrong.

- You will do anything for your significant other, even if you have to sacrifice your own needs and despite feeling unhappy or uncomfortable.

- You feel like you have to give up who you are to make your relationships work.

- You don't feel good about yourself unless other people like you.

CHAPTER 6

Codependency Vs. Dependency In Relationships

If you find yourself an enabler in a codependent relationship, you may also wonder what separates dependence from codependency within the relationship.

Keep in mind that partners, especially those in committed relationships like marriages, will be dependent upon each other for companionship, emotional support, and shared decision-making.

This is different from codependency, and the following examples provide further explanation of the difference between codependence vs. dependence:

With dependency, both people in the relationship rely upon each other for support and enjoy the relationship.

With codependency, the "taker" gets satisfaction out of having all of their demands met by their codependent partner. The "giver" is only happy with themselves if they sacrifice themselves to make their partner happy.

In a dependent relationship, both the partners prioritize their relationship and have outside interests, friends, and activities.

In codependent relationships, on the other hand, the codependent personality has no interests outside of the relationship.

In dependent relationships, both partners are allowed to express their desires and have their emotional needs met.

In codependent relationships, one partner sacrifices their requirements for the other person's sake, making the relationship entirely one-sided.

Why Is Codependency Unhealthy?

While being dependent upon a long-term partner is healthy and even acceptable, codependent relationships are unhealthy because the level of dependence is extreme.

The codependent personality sacrifices themself and loses their entire sense of identity for the sake of their partner. To be healthy, a person needs to balance caring for their partner with caring for their own needs. Codependency, on the other hand, becomes abusive and destructive.

The toxic nature of codependent relationships has been demonstrated in research. For instance, one study found that codependent family members of drug users suffered physically and emotionally.

Codependency within the family was linked to self-neglect and poor health, providing evidence that the codependent personality is not ideal. Giving up your own needs for the sake of someone else is not healthy, and remember that you cannot care for others if you do not first care for yourself.

How Does a Codependent Relationship Develop?

The patterns we demonstrate in our adult relationships are often a replication of what was learned during childhood.

If a person were emotionally neglected during childhood, they would accept emotional neglect in their relationships, leading to codependency.

Some specific ways that codependent relationships develop are as follows:

- A person experiences poor parenting, such as being taught that parents' needs are primary and their own needs do not matter.

- A person who ends up in codependent relationships may have suffered abuse and learned to repress their emotions to cope with the pain, leading them to neglect their own needs in relationships or seek out abusive partners.

- Someone may grow up with an ill parent and create a habit of caring for others, so this is the only way they know how to behave in relationships.

Fixing Codependent Behavior

If you recognize that you are involved in a codependent relationship, changing behavior is the first step in fixing codependent behavior.

Changing behavior requires conscious awareness and acknowledgment that there is a problem.

If you are struggling with codependency, the following strategies can be helpful:

1. Consider a hobby

Engage in a hobby outside of your relationship. Maybe you enjoy exercising, or you're interested in learning a new skill.

Whatever it may be, doing something just for you can help you to develop interests that do not revolve around your partner.

2. Set boundaries

Set boundaries with your partner. If you are in a codependent relationship, your entire day probably revolves around meeting your partner's needs and being at their beck and call.

If you want to fix this behavior, you must set boundaries. For instance, you may tell your partner that you have a specific schedule and that you will only be available at specified times of the day to take a phone call or help them.

3. Have a discussion

Have an honest discussion with your partner about the unhealthy nature of the relationship.

Please acknowledge that you are at fault for getting all of your happiness out of meeting their needs and expressing that your partner has enabled you by allowing you to plan your entire life around making them happy.

The two of you will have to work together to correct this pattern.

4. Say "No"

When you genuinely cannot do something for someone else or don't want to, practice saying, "No."

You have a right to turn things down that don't appeal to you or do not work for you.

5. Go out with friends

Spend time with friends. Your significant other becomes your priority in any committed relationship, but it is still important to have friendships.

Spending time with others will help you to create some natural separation from your partner.

6. Think positively about yourself

Practice positive affirmations. People who fall victim to codependent behavior tend to be critical of themselves, as they have low self-esteem. This creates the need for them to seek validation by being needed by other people.

Practice speaking positively to yourself, and you will find that you need less approval from others.

7. Join a support group

Consider attending a support group.

8. Stand up for yourself

Practice being assertive when someone tries to control you or disrespect you. People with a codependent personality tend to walk on eggshells to avoid upsetting other people, which can ultimately undermine their self-esteem.

The next time someone is unfair to you or tries to control you without your consent, stand up for your needs.

9. End the relationship

If you have experienced physical or emotional abuse from your partner, and your partner makes no effort to change, leaving a codependent relationship may be the best option for your safety and well-being.

10. Get professional help

Seek out therapy. Suppose you are unable to manage symptoms of codependency with the steps above.

In that case, you may benefit from codependency treatment to help you develop healthier coping strategies and work through past issues that have led to codependent relationships.

A therapist can help you to identify patterns from your childhood or family of origin so that you can overcome them and experience fulfilling, reciprocal relationships with others.

So, codependent relationships describe any relationship in which one person derives their happiness, self-esteem, and sense of worth from being needed by the other person.

The other member of the partnership enables codependent behavior by allowing their partner to make extreme sacrifices for their benefit. This type of behavior is often learned during childhood and continued in adult relationships, and it can be rather distressing.

Fortunately, there are ways to overcome codependency, ranging from spending more time with supportive friends to seeking codependency therapy from a professional.

CHAPTER 7

Codependency and Narcissism

Much of self-help literature portrays codependency and narcissism as polar opposites. Codependency is often associated with excess selflessness. Narcissistic personality disorder (NPD) is often linked to excess selfishness.

Many narratives depict codependent people as victims who fall prey to those with narcissistic traits. This oversimplification neglects a core truth at the heart of both codependency and narcissism: both codependents and narcissists can lack a healthy sense of self.

Codependency and Narcissism: Same Needs, Different Behaviors

Narcissism and codependency are both linked to an undefined self. They often struggle to get a sense of who they truly are. People with these conditions often rely on other people to define their own identities. As such, they place a lot of importance on what others think of them.

People with NPD often develop an intense, almost exclusive focus on themselves. They may display a lack of empathy or regard for others' needs. They may only care about others' feelings in relation to themselves. Narcissistic people often need someone else to inflate their self-esteem. They may need a continuous stream of affection and admiration to feel good about themselves. Some sources refer to this stream as a "narcissistic supply."

Meanwhile, people with codependency are often hyper-focused on others. They typically form an identity around serving others' needs. They may try to control another person's behavior, believing they know what is best for the person. Instead of praise, codependents often crave gratitude and a sense of "being needed."

Almost everyone wants to feel loved or important. Narcissism and codependency are two strategies to achieve that goal. However, both conditions can create an excessive reliance on others' approval.

The Common Origins of Codependency and Narcissism

Both codependency and narcissism are linked to adverse childhood experiences. A 2001 study of 793 mothers and children found a threefold increase in NPD among children whose mothers were verbally abusive. A 1999 study of 200 college students linked codependent behaviors to childhood parentification. Parentification is when a child takes on a caretaker role for their parents or siblings, often due to neglect or abuse.

People with NPD and codependency often have similar childhood experiences. They've simply adopted different ways of adapting. For example, say a pair of twins grow up neglected. One sibling may develop a low self-esteem and learn they are only "worth something" if they are useful to others. They may grow into a codependent adult who is used to sacrificing their own needs. The second sibling might develop an inflated self-esteem as a protective mechanism. The neglect makes the child feel unimportant, so as a narcissistic adult, they may crave constant validation to prove their self-worth.

The codependent and narcissistic siblings may develop very different behaviors and personalities. But in both scenarios, trauma and a fractured sense of self are at the core of the problem.

Understanding the Dance of Narcissism and Codependency

People with codependency sometimes form relationships with people who have NPD. Typically the two partners develop complementary roles to fill each other's needs. The codependent person has found a partner they can pour their self into, and the narcissistic person has found someone who puts their needs first.

Narcissism and codependency aren't always opposites. The desire to feel needed is not that different from the desire to feel important.However, this dynamic can quickly become unhealthy. The codependent person may try to live vicariously through their larger-than-life partner. When their partner doesn't show enough gratitude for their service, the codependent person may feel resentment. Meanwhile, the narcissistic person often exploits their partner's people-pleasing tendencies for their own narcissistic supply. As their ego grows, their demands may increase, until the codependent person eventually burns out.

Even if they develop an abusive relationship, neither partner may try to leave. Both people may stay in an unhealthy situation for fear of being alone. Without help, this dynamic can grow increasingly toxic.

Can Codependency and Narcissism Overlap?

Narcissism and codependency aren't always opposites. The desire to feel needed is not that different from the desire to feel important. While many studies find lower rates of narcissism among people with codependency, some have actually found higher rates of narcissism among those with codependent traits.

A person who is codependent in one situation might be narcissistic in another. For instance, a person might become codependent in their marriage, serving their spouse's every need. Yet that same person may feel an unending need for respect and praise from their children. causing them to manifest narcissistic tendencies.

In some cases, an abusive person may try to gaslight a codependent partner into believing they are narcissistic. The abuser may sabotage any show of self-confidence by calling their partner "egotistical." Typical acts of self-care, such as taking days off or spending time with friends, may be labeled "selfish." The codependent person may believe these accusations and try to fix the relationship by ignoring their own needs. A person isolated from loved ones—who might offer a more objective view—is likely to falsely believe they are a narcissist.

The fact that all people display narcissistic or codependent traits on occasion can make it even more difficult for a person to decide if they're narcissistic, codependent, or both.

Can Therapy Help?

Codependency and narcissism can become pathological when they undermine a person's quality of life or cause the person to harm others. It may be time to seek help if you show the following signs:

- A history of relationships in which abuse has been present.
- Difficulty feeling close to others.
- Feelings of emptiness or low self-esteem.
- Feeling as if your identity depends on what others think of you.
- Feeling like others don't fully appreciate you or acknowledge your importance.
- Feeling like you are never properly thanked for all you have given up.

A therapist can help people with narcissism or codependency understand the root of their insecurities. In therapy, you can learn how to replace flawed coping mechanisms with healthier behaviors. Talking through your experiences can help you access to new ways of thinking and being.

CHAPTER 8

Why are codependents always attracted to people who end up hurting them?

Codependents typically don't have a lot of self esteem.

Codependents often enter into relationships with people who are controlling or manipulative. These dominant partners of codependents are often self focused, lacking due concern for others' needs and failing to defer to others when they should.

The relationship is unhealthy for the codependent because they are not given the respect they may deserve.

There are a number of reasons why these relationships are sustained.

- Codependents sometimes stay in these relationships because don't respect themselves or don't have a high opinion of themselves. Sometimes they don't think they can do any better, so they don't break up and look for other relationships. Sometimes they don't think they deserve someone better — because they feel there is something inherently wrong with them.

- They don't have the sense of independence that most people do, and like having a dominant figure in their lives. It gives shape to their lives. Many codependents' lives don't have a firm sense of direction or shape, because they have a pattern of not having their own needs met and deferring to others' needs.

- They either don't understand or don't like who they are — and they like being in the presence of someone who can either tell them who they should be or could be, or how they should or could behave. They either want to improve, want to understand who they are, or want to be whoever the person they are dating wants them to be — and they believe that their life will be happier if they achieve these goals.

- They like the thrill of being around someone who is high status. People like to compensate for their flaws. If someone has low self esteem, being around someone who has extremely high self esteem can feel great — almost like a void being filled. This holds true even if the person with high self esteem doesn't always treat them that well. They don't feel great about themselves and it can be nice to be around people who are extremely pleased with themselves. It can feel like a rush.

- One definition of a codependent relationship is that the relationship is more important to the person than they are to themselves. If you go into a relationship with that sort of mindset, you'll subject yourself to considerable abuse.

- Codependence can also be caused by an unusual tendency to be very compliant. In general, if people are very compliant they will put up with a lot — even people treating them badly.

- Denial is often involved, as codependents often don't want to admit reality, and this leads them to stay in relationships too long and leads to situations where they get hurt.

- They have a victim mentality, so they frame the situation as one where they were the victim, rather than admitting their role in causing the unhealthy situation and learning from it.

CHAPTER 9

A Codependent Man

We throw around the word "codependency" without really knowing what it means. Alcoholics Anonymous coined the term in the 1970s to describe include a co-addict, or codependent, usually the overly controlling wife of an alcoholic man. Clinicians expanded this flawed definition in the mid-1980s to include both men and women with insecure attachment styles—anyone who cannot cope with the ending a relationship or losing control, even when the relationships is objectively unhealthy. But the prejudice stuck and, at least in the popular imagination, men are seldom called "codependent", even if the shoe fits.

"Women who are codependent often engage in people-pleasing behaviors, but so do men," said Sal Raichbach, a therapist at Ambrosia Treatment Centers. "However, there are some subtle differences."

Here's how to know whether you're a codependent man:

You Want To Rescue People

While women's codependency can manifest in the form of extreme caretaking, codependent men are drawn to people who seem like they need saving. "Men tend to be rescuers more than women," Raichbach says. "And sometimes codependent behavior displays itself as doing too much for their spouse, friend, or family member." This is not necessarily a bad thing but, when men are helping at the expense of their own well-being, this impulse could be coming from an unhealthy place. If you have to constantly be saving someone to feel content in a relationship, then you may be a codependent man.

Do You Make Sacrifices in Relationships That Others Don't

Making sacrifices is part of every healthy relationship, but if you find yourself making concessions that others aren't, then there may be a problem, according to psychologist Fran Walfish. People in [codependent relationships] believe that they're helping each other, but they don't have clean, clear, separate boundaries of where one person begins and the other person ends.

You Cover for Each Other, In Unhealthy Ways

It's understandable to want to trust your partner with your deepest, darkest secrets, and that you want to be there for them in a tough spot. But if you're covering for them to the extent that they never learn from their mistakes, you're less supporting and more enabling their bad behavior. This particular warning sign strikes at the heart of AA's original use of the term. The other person doesn't get the opportunity to learn from the experience. And that means the helpful behavior is no longer really helpful.

You Struggle With Things Just Being Fine

Codependent people tend to be most comfortable in states of hyperarousal, multiple studies suggest. If relationships are only comfortable for you when they're dramatic, it could be that you're uncomfortable when your relationship just fine. And that's often less because you crave conflict and more because drama alleviates that anxiety of having to deal with yourself on a normal, uneventful Tuesday. Indeed, studies suggest that people with a history of trauma are more likely to display codependent behavior. Perhaps because codependency is, if nothing else, a way of running away from yourself.

You're Defined by Your Relationship

Codependency is so difficult to detect because the sacrifices they make can easily be mistaken for healthy expressions of love. For men, who are historically less prone to commitment, being defined by a significant other seems like a romantic, even noble way to go against the grain. The problem is that holding relationships accountable for your identity doesn't work and only leads to an exhausting and unhealthy way of connecting with someone you clearly care a lot about. Needing another person that much makes for a good love song, but ultimately a bad relationship.

"Codependency a supportive, but distortive relationship," Walfish notes. "It's not a healthy way of relating and each person needs to be an independent, total, complete self."

The Problems Faced by Codependent Men

The dilemmas of codependent men aren't talked about. Unlike women, few men discuss their relationship problems with friends and family. Instead, they internalize their pain. Many are in denial, suffer in silence, have an addiction and/or become numb to their needs and feelings. They shun attention and try to do the right thing and be good sons, husbands, and fathers, focusing instead on making a living and meeting the needs of their wives and children. These codependent men sacrifice themselves and believe that their needs, including the need for time away from their wives, are selfish.

Societal and cultural values have shamed men as weak for expressing feelings or needs, which reinforces codependent traits of control, suppression of feelings, and denial of needs. Often, they turn to addiction in order to cope.

Dysfunctional Childhood

The societal norm for male suppression of feelings is compounded and distorted if you grew up in a dysfunctional family where it wasn't safe to express feelings and needs. It's easier not to acknowledge feelings that are criticized or needs that are denied or shamed. Your needs were also ignored if you took on age-inappropriate responsibilities because of an out of control, irresponsible, or immature parent. If there was abuse or addiction present, you probably grew up in an atmosphere of chaos, conflict, strict rules, or unpredictability. Self-control helped you survive, but controlling yourself or others leads to problems later in intimate relationships.

Feeling Trapped and Fearing Abandonment

Despite the prevalence of codependent women, I see many codependent men in my private practice. There's a dance that codependent couples do, and it takes two who know the steps. If you think your wife is codependent, there's a good chance you are, too. Often codependent men are attracted to women who are needy, demanding, jealous, or critical. Men become dependent on their wives' approval, and then feel trapped by their manipulation, demands, or expectations. Some are involved with women who are abusive, or never satisfied or appreciative. They're unable to set boundaries and fear emotional retaliation and/or rejection, including withholding of sex.

Their wives may be very emotional, providing a sense of aliveness to the relationship and compensating for the numbness many codependent men feel inside. In the beginning, a man can feel powerful, helping a needy girlfriend or wife and giving her attention or gifts. He conforms to her expectations, while being assured that she won't abandon him, but eventually discovers that it's never enough to satisfy her. Sometimes, these women have mental health issues, are addicted to drugs or alcohol, or are financially desperate.

Some men end up becoming workaholics to justify alone time, but their needs for nurturing, respect, freedom, and appreciation, just to name a few, go unmet. Fear of rejection and abandonment are powerful motivators for codependency, usually because of early emotional abandonment by a parent. Consequently, the men never leave — physically — but withdraw to the safety of a self-made emotional prison. After a while, they feel trapped, controlled, and resentful. They may use drugs or addictive behavior to manage anxiety and depression, while some look outside the marriage for validation. However, it's not their wives that are the cause of their problem, it's their codependency.

Intimacy

Frequently, a woman brings her partner into therapy wanting more intimacy and to get him to be more open and share his feelings. Often, it's revealed that he's fully capable of communicating his feelings, but instead of being assertive and setting healthy boundaries that make it safe for him to do so, he reacts to criticism and demands by fighting back, emotionally withdrawing, or endlessly placating her with explanations and apologies that don't suffice.

Codependent couples are reactive because they each lack autonomy and are emotionally dependent upon each other. Problems of closeness and separateness are typical. Couples may keep a safe distance or take turns pushing one another away to avoid the emotional intensity of becoming too close. Intimacy escalates anxiety of being hurt by criticism or rejection or being suffocated and losing themselves and their autonomy. Yet, despite unhappiness or frustration, they don't leave and draw each other in after a conflict or separation, so as not to be abandoned.

Abused Men

Some men are verbally and even physically abused by their wives and girlfriends and don't know how to handle it. Often, they're afraid that authorities won't believe that their wives are violent and feel humiliated and ashamed that they can't deal with it themselves. Sometimes, their wives threaten to lie, or do so, and accuse their partners of violence. These men keep their secret and suffer silently. They can learn to value themselves and change the relationships dynamics by healing their codependency and setting boundaries.

Codependency and Addiction

Men who are addicts are also codependent. Their lives revolve around their addiction — whether it's a drug (including alcohol), sex, gambling, food, or work — which they use to modulate their mood and self-esteem. They try to control their addiction and people around them in order to maintain the addiction. Meanwhile, they are controlled by it. Abstinence or sobriety allows them to work on the underlying issues of codependency. Recovery includes regaining autonomy and self-esteem, and the ability to manage their thinking, emotions and life problems.

CHAPTER 10

Myths Men Need to Know About Codependency

Codependency exists on a continuum, and isn't always all or nothing. I don't love the term codependency.

It's often misunderstood; some people find it a helpful description and others think it feels blaming or inaccurate. Unfortunately, there isn't another succinct way of describing what are commonly described as codependent traits.

Some people seem to think everyone's codependent. In an effort to bring some clarity to the term codependency,

I want to address some of the common myths about codependency.

Myth 1: Codependency means being really nice and helpful

Codependency isn't just being really nice and helpful.

One of the hallmark traits of codependency is care-taking and a strong desire to please and help others. However, codependency is much more. For people with codependent traits, the strong desire to help also serves as a way to feel needed and important; it's central to their identity. For people with codependency, helping and fixing also involve an element of trying to control and change people and situations in order to manage their anxiety, discomfort, and feeling out of control.

Codependents don't feel very good about themselves and caretaking is a way to feel needed and important, which is why they feel compelled to do it even when it's to their own detriment.

Myth #2: Codependency only happens in families with an alcoholic family member

Codependency doesn't only develop in families dealing with addiction.

It's true that the concept of codependency originally came from trying to understand the dynamics of women married to alcoholic men. However, as our understanding has grown over the years, we've come to recognize that codependency can develop in a wide array of family situations. People with codependent traits often grew up in families with addiction, untreated mental illness, abuse, or neglect. But there are still others with codependent traits who describe growing up in well-functioning families. These families may have set exceptionally high standards, not been attentive to emotional needs, or emphasized caring for others or pleasing others over taking care of oneself and developing a strong, independent self.

Myth #3: You're either codependent or you're not

Codependency isn't all or nothing.

You can have codependent traits to varying degrees. You may have only a few codependent traits or you may have many. And you may feel the impact of them to varying degrees. For some people codependent traits cause significant problems in their lives and for other people they don't (although it's important to note that this could be denial). Codependency isn't a mental health diagnosis so there isn't a definitive diagnostic criterion. Think of codependency as existing on a continuum.

Myth #4: Codependents are weak and create dysfunctional relationships

You didn't develop codependent because you're weak. Quite the contrary: people with codependent traits are strong—so very strong. They are survivors. Codependency is a natural and understandable reaction to trauma, overwhelming experiences, or inattentive or inconsistent parenting. Codependent traits develop as a way to cope. They're adaptive and strong.

Codependency isn't your fault. You aren't the cause of your dysfunctional relationships. Relationship problems are the result of all the people involved. Sometimes people with codependent traits think "I should be able to make my spouse (or child or parent) stop drinking. If I was stronger (or smarter or prettier), s/he'd stop." This is flawed thinking that leaves you blaming yourself and trying to control the uncontrollable.

When you acknowledge your codependent traits, you take ownership of your own thoughts and behaviors. Accepting your codependent traits doesn't mean you are responsible for being mistreated or for anyone else's poor choices or behaviors. And while many people with codependent traits are the victims of abuse and trauma, accepting your part in the relationship dynamics does not in any way justify or mean that you're responsible for being abused or mistreated.

Myth #5: You'll always be codependent

If you choose to make changes, you won't always have codependent traits.

Thought patterns and behavior patterns can be changed. It can be a lengthy process, but people absolutely change their patterns. I believe that acknowledging your codependent traits is the place to begin. As I said, I know that some people don't like the term codependency and feel it's blaming, but I think it can be empowering if you choose to make it so. When you know how your thoughts and behaviors aren't serving you well, you can begin to change them.

You can start untangling yourself from the unhealthy people and relationships in your life.

You can become emotionally free.

CHAPTER 11

Your Responsibility For Your Partner's Recovery as a Man

A new study is making the rounds of professionals in recovery centers about how men behave when they reach the codependent stage of a relationship. It describes the family therapy that men should receive when their partners are in rehab treatment. Authors Dan Griffin and Rick Dauer have published "Rethinking Men and Codependency" in the online Addiction Professional journal, and they express some surprising viewpoints about male codependency and addiction.

Some Codependency Is Natural

The first posit is that codependency makes up a natural part of any relationship—that all relationships comprise independent, interdependent, and codependent interactions. However, based on the theory that men lack skills in relationship maintenance, their codependency often manifests in ugly and undesirable ways.

The authors assert that we all benefit from some level of codependency in our relationships. If codependency means that we take away a good feeling from the fact of the relationship, there is no harm in some level of codependency. The negativity of codependency comes when relationships are defined by one partner's self-worth based upon the behavior of the other partner.

In terms of addiction, this means that the male codependent feels validated when he responds to save the addict from herself. Since addiction can be such an all-consuming force in the life of the addict—and the people around her—it's not long before her partner gets sucked into an ever-widening spiral of codependency that obliterates the balancing forces of independence and interdependence.

The Male Behavioral Model

The next posit of the authors surrounds the behaviors that boys are taught as they grow into men: Don't cry. Be tough. Never give way. Don't ask for help.

Men generally do not work to sustain relationships in the same way as women. They are not good at interpersonal skills like communication, conflict resolution, setting healthy boundaries, identifying personal needs, self-care, emotional expression, intimacy, or a willingness to ask for help.

Codependence can generate feelings of being powerless, vulnerable, fearful, and insecure. But men express those feelings with arrogance or detachment. They are good at hollering and raging around the house. They are manipulative and controlling or even paternalistic.

When Codependency Takes Over

If you are the male half of a relationship in which your partner is using alcohol or drugs, your codependent behaviors will soon become the dominant part of your relationship. By their very nature, you are most likely to express your feelings by avoiding intimacy or cheating outside of your relationship. Your actions toward your addicted partner will involve verbal abuse and threats. You will watch her carefully and try to control everything she does. Your fear of abandonment—nobody wants a relationship to end simply because of addiction—could result in a lasting distrust in your own instincts and a cynicism toward others.

CHAPTER 12

Signs Your Partner Is Codependent

Codependent relationships can be detrimental to both people.

Maintaining a healthy relationship is hard. Many times, issues that may cause problems later, manifest themselves without a couple even realizing. Codependency is one such issue. Codependency is excessive emotional or psychological reliance on a partner.

A person can become codependent because of how they were raised. Dysfunctional families or growing up with an ill parent is likely to create codependent behavior. Of course, being raised in a dysfunctional family by no means guarantees you will be codependent later in life, but for some, it can create this pattern.

Signs of a codependent partner are not always obvious to spot. Oftentimes, the codependent behavior makes the other partner feel good so there is no incentive for them to interfere. The codependent partner has to separate and develop their own self-esteem or leave the relationship for both people to get better.

Here are 10 ways to tell if your partner is too codependent.

1. They can't say no, ever

It can be difficult for a codependent person to say "no." It's one thing to do something nice for someone you care about, but it's another to feel like you always have to.

Codependents don't feel they have a choice. Saying 'no' causes them anxiety so they go out of their way to sacrifice their needs to accommodate other.

2. They never feel like they're good enough for you

It can be hard for a codependent person to accept that they can be loved for who they really are.

Oftentimes, a codependent partner in a relationship will exhibit low self-esteem. They don't feel a strong sense of self-worth which is one of the reasons they are always aiming to please.

For this reason, codependents tend to not express their true feelings or what they're really thinking out of fear that their partner may abandon them.

3. They feel responsible for you

Codependents put others first. Codependent partners are willing to make extreme sacrifices to make their partner happy. They will go above and beyond to meet their partner's needs no matter what it takes.

Codependents put others first, which sounds altruistic, but when it's at the cost of your own well-being they are doing more harm for themselves than good.

4. They get upset when they don't hear from you

Codependents might have a strong fear of abandonment.

If a codependent feels any type of abandonment, even if it's something as small as not getting a call from their partner when they said they would, they can quickly shut down.

This is due to their high levels of fear of abandonment. Suddenly, every worst-case scenario about what could have happened to their significant other is running through their head, when in reality their partner is fine.

5. They can't enjoy themselves without you

They might only feel safe around you. Chances are, if you're in a serious relationship you and your partner have "couple friends," but it's important to also have your own friends, too.

Codependent partners have trouble enjoying life outside of their relationship because they feel safer, more in control, and confident when they're with their significant other.

6. They fixate on their mistakes

Mistakes might feel like a big deal to codependents.

We all mess up in relationships, but the important thing is to forgive each other and move on.

Codependent partners fixate on their mistakes. The reason for this, is that a codependent needs other people's approval to feel good about themselves and if they mess up, or make a mistake, they feel anxiety and stress of abandonment.

7. They have poor personal boundaries

Codependents feel responsible for others which leads to weak personal boundaries.

Many times, a codependent partner is so crippled, knowingly or not, by the fear of abandonment, the fear that they'll jeopardize the relationship, or won't be liked, that they have a hard time setting boundaries for themselves — physical or emotional.

8. They must always be in control

Being in control helps codependents feel safe and secure. Obviously, we all want to have some amount of control over our lives, but for a codependent partner, staying in control keeps them from having to take risks or share their true feelings.

All the people pleasing and caretaking is a form of control as well. It may be subconscious, but being extra nice and a people-pleaser helps codependents manipulate people and situations the way they feel they need to be.

9. They're very indecisive

They likely don't want to upset their partner.

From what to have for dinner to whether or not to take a job offer, a codependent is not good about making decisions, no matter how trivial. They rely so heavily on their partner's opinions and feelings towards them that they'd rather not have an opinion as not to upset their partner if they should disagree.

They're afraid to be truthful because they don't want to upset anyone.

10. They can't stand not being there for you when you need

It goes back to their feelings of needing to be in control.

We all want to be there for the people we love but sometimes life gets in the way and we can't. If a codependent can't be there for their partner, they can feel very distressed.

This all goes back to the feeling of being in control and low self-esteem. If someone else is helping out their partner in need, no matter how silly the need may be, it will make them feel inadequate.

Ultimately codependents must find themselves on their own.

Healthy interdependence is the key.

It's a misconception to think you can "fix" a codependent relationship. Codependency is a disorder of the self. You can only work on changing yourself. That's why it's important to practice detachment from your partner to become more autonomous and less reactive.

Healthy interdependence is the key. That means that you are emotionally available for your partner but do not rely on them for your feelings of love and overall well-being. We believe that independence is the healthiest state of being when, in reality, a healthy relationship with good interdependence is what we should be striving for.

The goal is to focus on yourself. Trying to change your partner is a sign of your own codependency, and the opposite is actually necessary – focus on yourself. When one partner changes, the entire dynamic shifts, and the other partner changes too, by necessity.

CHAPTER 13

Fixing an Addicted and Codependent Relationship

For a very long time, I could not decipher between codependency and love. I thought that if we love someone, we put that person's needs before ours and make their happiness our business.

It is true that love is unselfish. When we have children, their needs have to come before ours. We are not going to let our baby cry for hours from hunger in the middle of the night because we feel like sleeping. We will drive our children around to activities when we are tired or would rather be doing something else. Acting responsibly as a parent is part of what it means to love our children.

However, when we always put the other first in our adult relationships, at the expense of our own health or well-being, we may be codependent.

The Relationship Between Codependency and Addiction

One of the many problems with a codependent relationship is that you may be inadvertently enabling a partner's addiction. In your attempt to show your love by "helping" your partner, you can discourage him or her from seeking the treatment necessary to get sober.

For example:

- You justify your husband's drinking by saying he has had a stressful day or needs to relax.
- You make excuses when your girlfriend can't come to social functions because she is under the influence of heroin.
- You let your boyfriend borrow your prescription opioids whenever he complains of any minor discomfort, even though you're worried about his growing dependence on the medication.

- You quietly take on extra responsibilities around the house or in parenting your children because your partner is always under the influence.
- You find yourself frequently apologizing to others or doing favors to repair relationships damaged by your partner's drug or alcohol abuse.
- You risk your own financial future by loaning money to your partner to cover debts incurred from substance abuse.

Addiction impairs judgement and critical thinking skills. This makes it very difficult for someone with a substance use disorder to see that they need help. When you go out of your way to prevent your partner from experiencing the consequences of substance abuse, you make it less likely that they will acknowledge that a problem exists.

Loving someone with a substance use disorder can also cause your codependent tendencies to spiral out of control. When your partner is behaving erratically due to drug or alcohol abuse, it's easy to resort to using codependent behavior in your fight to maintain a sense of control over chaotic surroundings. This creates a vicious cycle that traps both of you in a dysfunctional and unhealthy relationship.

Healing from Codependency

The good news is that codependency is a learned behavior, which means it can be unlearned. If you love your partner and want to keep the relationship, you need to heal yourself first and foremost.

Some healthy steps to healing your relationship from codependency include:

- **Start being honest with yourself and your partner.** Doing things that we do not want to do not only wastes our time and energy, but it also brings on resentments. Saying things that we do not mean only hurts us, because we then are living a lie. Be honest in your communication and in expressing your needs and desires.
- **Stop negative thinking.** Catch yourself when you begin to think negatively. If you begin to think that you deserve to be treated badly, catch yourself and

change your thoughts. Be positive and have higher expectations.

- **Don't take things personally.** It takes a lot of work for a codependent person not to take things personally, especially when in an intimate relationship. Accepting the other as they are without trying to fix or change them is the first step.

- **Take breaks.** There is nothing wrong with taking a break from your partner. It is healthy to have friendships outside of your partnership. Going out with friends brings us back to our center, reminding us of who we really are.

- **Consider counseling.** Get into counseling with your partner. A counselor serves as an unbiased third party. They can point out codependent tendencies and actions between the two of you that you may not be aware of. Feedback can provide a starting point and direction. Change cannot happen if we do not change.

- **Establish boundaries.** Those who struggle with codependency often have trouble with boundaries.

We do not know where our needs begin or where the other's end. We often thrive off guilt and feel bad when we do not put the other first.

Self-Care Is Not Selfish

As you're working to break the cycle of codependency, it may seem like you are being encouraged to behave in a way that is selfish and unfair to your partner. This couldn't be further from the truth.

In a healthy relationship, both people have fully formed identities outside of their time together. They each bring unique attributes to the table—creating a partnership that allows both of them to grow and thrive.

Watching a loved one struggle with drug or alcohol addiction is heartbreaking, but you won't be in any position to support your partner's addiction treatment unless you make time to address your own mental health needs.

CHAPTER 14

How to Stop Being Codependent

Codependency is often referred to as "relationship addiction." It's an emotional and behavioral condition that interferes with an individual's ability to develop a healthy, mutually satisfying relationship. It can be frustrating and destructive, but there are things that you can do to learn how to stop being codependent.

Examples of Codependency

Here are some examples of what a codependent relationship might look like:

In parent-child relationships it can involve:

- Doing everything for an adult child who should be independent
- Getting a sense of meaning or purpose from financially supporting an adult child
- Never allowing a child do to anything independently
- Dropping everything to care for a parent
- Neglecting other responsibilities and relationships to respond to parents' demands
- Never talking about problems in family relationships or behaviors

In romantic relationships it can involve:

- Investing a lot of energy and time into caring for a partner with an alcohol or substance abuse problem
- Making excuses or covering for the other person's bad behavior
- Neglecting self-care, work, or other relationships to care for your partner

- Enabling a partner's destructive or unhealthy behavior

- Not allowing your partner to take responsibility for their own lives

- Not allowing your partner to maintain their independence

Why It Happens

Codependency is learned by watching and imitating other family members who display this type of behavior. It's often passed down from one generation to the next. So a child who grew up watching a parent in a codependent relationship may repeat the pattern.

Codependency occurs in dysfunctional families where members often experience anger, pain, fear, or shame that is denied or ignored. Underlying issues that contribute to the dysfunction may involve:

- Addiction to drugs, alcohol, work, food, sex, gambling, relationships

- Abuse (physical, emotional, or sexual)

- Chronic physical illness or mental illness

Problems within the family are never confronted. Codependent individuals don't bring up the fact that issues exist. Family members repress their emotions and disregard their own needs in an effort to care for the individual who is struggling.

All of the attention and energy goes toward the individual who is abusive, ill, or addicted. The codependent individual usually sacrifices all of their own needs to care for the family member who is struggling. They usually experience social, emotional, and physical consequences as they disregard their own health, welfare, and safety.

Risk Factors and Characteristics

While anyone might find themselves in a codependent relationship, there are certain factors that increase the risk. Researchers have identified several factors that are often linked with codependency:

- Lack of trust in self or others
- Fear of being alone or abandoned
- A need to control other people
- Chronic anger

- Frequent lying

- Poor communication skills

- Trouble making decisions

- Problems with intimacy

- Difficulty establishing boundaries

- Trouble adjusting to change

- An extreme need for approval and recognition

- A tendency to become hurt when others don't recognize their efforts

- An inclination to do more than their share all the time

- A tendency to confuse love and pity

- An exaggerated sense of responsibility for the actions of others

Studies show codependency is common in adults who were raised by parents with substance abuse problems, who live in chronic stressful family environments, who have children with behavior problems, and who care for the chronically ill. Women are more likely to be codependent than men.

Individuals in the helping professions are also more likely to be in codependent relationships. It's estimated that one-third of nurses have moderate to severe levels of codependency. Nurses need to be sensitive to the needs of others and often need to set aside their own feelings for the good of their patients. They may also find validation in their ability to care for others, and that need may spill over into their personal lives.

Identifying Codependent Relationships

While codependency isn't something that shows up in a lab test or a brain scan, there are some questions that you can ask yourself to help spot codependent behavior.

- Do you feel compelled to help other people?
- Do you try to control events and how other people should behave?
- Are you afraid to let other people be who they are and allow events to happen naturally?
- Do you feel ashamed of who you are?

- Do you try to control events and people through helplessness, guilt, coercion, threats, advice-giving, manipulation, or domination?

- Do you have a hard time asking others for help?

- Do you feel compelled or forced to help people solve their problems (i.e., offering advice)?

- Do you often hide what you are really feeling?

- Do you avoid openly talking about problems?

- Do you push painful thoughts and feelings out of your awareness?

- Do you blame yourself and put yourself down?

If you answer yes to many of these questions, it may be a sign of codependent behavior patterns in your relationships. Identifying these patterns is an important step in learning how to stop being codependent.

Some individuals are able to overcome codependency on their own. Learning about what it means to be codependent and the harm it causes can be enough for some individuals to change their behavior. Some steps you can take to overcome codependence include:

- **Look for signs of a healthy relationship.** In order to break out of codependent patterns, you need to first understand what a healthy, loving relationship looks like. Signs of a healthy relationship include making time for each other, maintaining independence, being honest and open, showing affection, and having equality.

- **Having healthy boundaries.** People with good relationships are supportive of each other, but they also respect each other's boundaries. A boundary is a limit that establishes what you are willing and unwilling to accept in a relationship. Spend some time thinking about what is acceptable to you. Work on listening to the other person, but don't allow their problems to consume your life. Practice finding ways to decline requests that step over your boundaries. Set limits, then work on enforcing them.

- **Take care of yourself.** People who are in codependent relationships often have low self-esteem. In order to stop being codependent, you need to start by valuing yourself. Learn more about the things that make you happy and the kind of life that you want to live. Spend time doing the things that you love to do. Work on overcoming negative self-talk and replace self-defeating thoughts with more positive, realistic ones. Also, be sure that you are taking care of your health by getting the food, rest, and self-care that you need for your emotional well-being.

Some people learn about their codependent tendencies through books or articles. Others stop being codependent when they experience environmental changes, such as when a partner becomes sober or they get a new job that requires them to stop care-taking.

Getting Help

Codependency often requires professional treatment, however. It can be treated with talk therapy. Research shows that several different types of therapy treatments can be effective in improving the quality of one's life and learning how to stop being codependent.

Group Therapy

There are several different group interventions that may be effective for codependency. The group dynamic gives individuals an opportunity to form healthier relationships in an appropriate space. Group therapy often involves giving positive feedback and holding individuals accountable.

Group therapy methods may vary. Some involve cognitive behavioral therapy, where members learn specific skill-building strategies.

Other codependency groups follow the 12-step model. Similar to the way other 12-step groups are run, individuals learn about their relationship addiction. Goals may include increasing self-awareness, self-esteem, and the expression of feelings.

Family Therapy

Family therapy targets the dysfunctional family dynamics. Family members learn how to recognize their dysfunctional patterns so they can learn how to improve their relationships.

Improved communication is often a key goal of family therapy. Issues that have never before been discussed in the family may be raised in therapy. Sometimes, one individual creates a change (such as getting sober or encouraging someone to be more independent) and it can change the entire family dynamic.

Cognitive Therapy

Cognitive therapy can target the thoughts that contribute to unhealthy relationship patterns. For example, an individual who thinks, "I can't stand being alone," is likely to go to great lengths to maintain the relationship, even when it's not healthy to do so. Therapy sessions might focus on learning how to tolerate uncomfortable emotions and changing irrational thoughts.

The goal is likely to create positive behavior changes and allow the other individual to accept more personal responsibility for their own actions.

Treatment may delve into a person's childhood, since most codependent individuals are patterning their relationships after ones they grew up seeing. Therapy may assist someone in getting in touch with their emotions and helping them experience a wide range of feelings again.

So, if you suspect you are codependent in your relationship and you're struggling to create positive change, seek professional help. You might start by talking to your doctor or you can reach out to a mental health professional directly about how to stop being codependent.

If you aren't comfortable speaking to a therapist in person or you are hesitant to attend a group, consider online therapy. You can speak to a therapist from the privacy of your own home from one of your electronic devices via video, live chat, or messaging.

CHAPTER 15

Steps on How to Break Codependency Habits

Now that you understand the impact of codependency, you may be more motivated to undergo the often-difficult task of overcoming it.

Below are five steps to help you on your journey:

Learn to love yourself

This is the catch-all solution for avoiding and overcoming codependency.

People who love and respect themselves have boundaries for the types of people they'll stay in relationships with. They won't crave affection from just anyone. They're able to leave a partner who isn't right for them and therefore won't fall in codependency.

However, if you suffered from a difficult upbringing, learning to love yourself may not be easy.

Below, are some practical steps to help you engage in self-love.

Write a self-love list

Complete a list of 50 things you love about yourself. Include past achievements, physical attributes, likable parts of your personality and anything else you can think of. Feel free to add weaknesses that you're attempting to improve upon, too. The fact you're bothering to better yourself at all makes this list-worthy.

Fifty is A LOT. The challenge is supposed to be difficult, so it forces you to dig deep and uncover everything you appreciate about yourself.

The result is a huge helping of self-love. Those who believe in the power of affirmations may want to read their list every day. Either way, the fact that you managed to write

50 items should provide a jolt of self-esteem during difficult moments.

Start a gratitude journal

If you start a gratitude journal, you'll be joining worldwide names such as Tony Robbins, Arianna Huffington, and Oprah Winfrey in doing so.

There are many forms of gratitude journals, but many people use it to list five things they're grateful for each morning and five achievements they're proud of every evening. Nothing is too insignificant to be listed.

Meditation

Meditation is the practice of staying in the present moment, rather than listening to your internal voices.

It's fantastic for improving focus, calming anxiety, and reducing stress. If your inner voices constantly remind you of your fears and insecurities, it could be a great habit for increasing your self-love too.

In fact, it's possible to focus your meditation on gratitude and self-love.

Develop hobbies and passions

If you find an activity you're truly passionate about, this will go a long way in stopping you from worrying about your relationship status.

The best hobbies for overcoming codependency are those you can engage in alone. Your passion should allow you to garner a flow state that makes the hours fly by without you even noticing.

Many athletes describe experiencing this sensation during sports. Musicians experience the same while practicing their instruments as do artists in the middle of their latest creation.

Your passion doesn't have to involve talent. It can be as simple as reading or listening to music, provided that it makes you satisfied in your own company. If you haven't found a passion, that's a fantastic excuse to try new activities. *Meetup.com* is a brilliant website, which will list plenty of ideas in your local area.

Of course, you can engage in hobbies with your friends, too. Just don't become too dependent on their company for a good time.

Gain romantic abundance

Most people fall into codependence because they feel their destructive relationship is their only chance for love. They cling to that unhealthy person because they believe noone else will have them.

As such, a great step for overcoming codependency is to gain romantic abundance. This might be a more long-winded step than the others, but it remains important.

If you're not currently abundant with romantic options, you may have to indulge in self-improvement and that's absolutely fine.

Learning to love yourself will do loads to gain you more romantic options. Indulging in hobbies, nurturing friendships, and leading a life that other people want to be a part of will also help. Making an effort to meet more people, whether that's through social events or dating apps like Tinder is another great idea.

You can work on your appearance, perhaps by exercising or updating your fashion. But it's the added confidence from the other steps listed above that'll do the most to attract more love interests into your life.

This work will make you less attached to lovers who are wrong for you and give you the ability to choose your best fit from a bigger field of people.

End your codependent relationship

Just as going cold turkey on cigarettes is the best solution for smokers, ending your unhealthy relationship is a key step for overcoming codependency.

A clean break from the relationship is crucial if you're serious about focusing on yourself in the way that this article advises.

You might think you're able to become the hero that 'saves' your partner from their codependent feelings, but it's harder than you think. You can only save people that want saving. Remember, most codependent lovers came from backgrounds where they only knew pain. No matter how much love you show them, they'll reject it, unless they're ready to change. Only they can make that decision.

A break-up is likely to be the best aid for your partner.

Scott Wetzler, psychology division chief at Albert Einstein College of Medicine, explains: "Sometimes people delude themselves into thinking they are helping a codependent partner by continuing to cater to his or her anxiety. But ask if you are truly helping or simply fostering that negativity."

Perhaps, in cases where marriage and children are involved, it's worth taking a shot at saving your relationship. In such situations, it's recommended to do so with the assistance of a professional relationship counselor.

Choose a new partner with high self-esteem

Once you've learned to love yourself and find happiness with or without a relationship, it's important to ensure any new partner has the same ability.

Be careful and look for signs of extreme neediness, jealousy or engaging in controlling behavior.

If you spot these red flags, call them out straight away. If these symptoms persist, break the relationship off. You deserve better.

The verdict

Codependency is probably more common than you realize, so don't beat yourself up if you fall into it.

However, it is important to be aware of its detrimental effects and to never to accept being part of a codependent relationship.

Overcoming codependency isn't easy, but it's well worth the effort to secure your long-term happiness.

CHAPTER 16

How to stop being codependent (Contd.)

So, you think that you may be codependent. Some of the signs sound a bit like you, and now you're wondering how to stop it.

First, let me say that the relationships you have that are codependent don't have to stop. Someone who loves you and values you as a person is going to want you to get help—without strings attached.

They're going to help you get better instead of pulling you down.

Some codependent relationships are toxic, and they'll always be that way. But many relationships are codependent solely because you're bringing your past into them, and they don't have to be that way.

When you stop being codependent, the relationships you have right now can be more fulfilled and stronger.

Here are the 15 easy ways to stop being codependent:

1. Figure out what is codependent in your relationship

You may not have every sign of codependency. Chances are, you have a pattern. So maybe you take everything upon yourself and feel like no one notices. Maybe you go above and beyond for everyone else but yourself.

Whatever it is that you're doing, figure it out. Look for the patterns in your relationship that are codependent behaviors. Keep a list and keep track of the things that you're doing. This will help you realize when you do something that should stop.

You can't stop being codependent if you don't know how you're being codependent. This is the first step for everyone.

Recognize your codependency. Don't shy away from it.

2. Know your self-worth

I get it.

This advice seems so obvious and cliche.

But to overcome codependency in a relationship, you have to work on the most important relationship you'll ever have in life — the one you have with yourself.

For many people, being codependent is a negative reflection of their self-worth.

And in this day and age it's harder to love yourself than it's ever been.

From a very young age we're conditioned to think happiness comes from the external.

That it's only when we discover the "perfect person" to be in a relationship with can we find self-worth, security and happiness.

I think this is a life-wrecking myth.

One which not only causes so many unhappy relationships, but also poisons you into living a life devoid of optimism and personal independence.

3. Set up boundaries

Once you've realized what it is that you're doing, stop and set boundaries. Realize that the things you are doing aren't helping you. You're hurting yourself.

Even though you're helping others, it's not helpful when you then rage about it a few weeks later. No one wants that.

Set boundaries for yourself. Accept help from others. Learn to say no. Stop doing everything for everyone around you.

4. Work through your past

Since so much of being codependent comes from your past, you'll need to work through it. This is something most people don't want to do. Being codependent often comes with that sense of denial.

We don't want to be codependent, so we think by ignoring it, it'll go away. But, that's not true. You have to work through all the crap in your life. And sometimes, there's stuff you don't even remember.

The past of a codependent individual is filled with unresolved conflicts dealing with love and emotional needs, with familial issues playing the biggest part of it.

Analyze your past, and try to remember the fuzzy parts that your mind might have repressed.

This exploration can be emotionally stressful and draining, but it's the essential first step before you can truly move forward.

When you meet to talk to a therapist, it's a safe place where you can discuss your past. You don't have to sugarcoat it or make it sound better than it was. And in that process, you may happen upon things you didn't even remember.

It's a very cathartic process, and as much as we think we might not need it, codependent people should absolutely see a therapist.

It's the most important and one of the only ways you can stop being codependent and have a better life.

5. Overcome denial

Be frank with yourself. Admit that your problems are real, and they were carried over from your unfulfilled childhood emotional needs.

The later in life that you sum up the courage to look your denial in the face and walk past it, the longer you will have to deal with dysfunctional relationships and hurting those trying to love you.

6. Detach, disentangle

Cut away from the person you are now and the dysfunctions that make up who you are.

Detach from your pains, your problems, your anxieties and your worries, and try to imagine a "new you" without the baggage and preoccupations of the past.

Try to envision the ideal relationship you want to have, and imagine the person you need to be to create a relationship like that?

What are the parts of you that need shedding away? What are the unfulfilled needs and deep-seated thoughts chaining you to the idiosyncrasies creating this suboptimal version of yourself?

Identify those issues, and every time you feel them again, do your best to recognize them and consider the situation a second time without those issues clouding your mind.

7. Learn to say no

A major issue with codependent individuals is the inability to prioritize the self — your needs and wants over the needs and wants of others.

Whereas emotionally functional people have clear boundaries, codependent individuals are afraid to put up any boundaries when dealing with other people, because they don't want to risk upsetting anyone or causing themselves to lose their relationship.

Understand your self-worth. Learn your boundaries and establish them, and protect these boundaries when dealing with other people.

Your boundaries are an extension of who you are, and by making those around you acknowledge and respect your boundaries, you indirectly make them acknowledge and respect you.

8. Find supportive people

Like I mentioned above, the people who truly love and care about you will stick by your side. The ones that don't probably aren't healthy for you. Toxic relationships shouldn't be kept in your life just because you think you're supposed to keep them.

Remove the toxicity and find supportive people. It may be a friend, spouse, parent, or just a therapist. It doesn't matter if you have a hundred supportive people or just one, that support person is going to be needed.

You don't stop being codependent overnight. It's a serious, deeply ingrained problem that is hard to get past. Support is everything.

9. Care for Yourself

Ultimately, overcoming codependency revolves around learning to care for yourself. You treat others with the caring and love that you yourself need, because you have difficulty believing that you deserve love without earning it.

Before anyone else can love you the way you need them to, you need to love yourself by establishing your value and self-worth.

And this begins with giving yourself the same compassion and care that you give those around you. Think about the things that you need for you to be happy, and protect your feelings and emotions from those who might be bringing you down. Learn to love yourself and be open with your own needs.

10. Put yourself first

You're so used to taking care of others that you've forgotten about yourself. You have to put yourself first. There's nothing better than self-love and self-care, especially when you've spent years thinking you don't deserve it.

One of the best ways to stop being codependent right now is to think about yourself. Go out and do something that you love. Stop doing all the housework and watch a TV show. Take a break. Take a bath. Eat some dessert. Do something!

Thinking of others first isn't a bad thing—but it can be exhausting when you're codependent. Try to remember that you are important. You are worthy. And you deserve to be put first as well.

11. Embrace honesty

Stop doing things that feel like a waste of your energy and time, because these lead to resentments between you and your partner.

Say the truth about what you feel, what you need, and give your partner the opportunity to make you truly happy.

12. Grow thicker skin

You have spent a lifetime having very little self-worth and self-esteem, so it's normal that you might be overly sensitive and easy to wilt at the slightest criticism or negativity.

Start learning how to continue moving through feelings and events that make you feel uncomfortable, and become a stronger version of yourself.

13. Take emotional breaks

When you need a break, you need a break. Whether it's a break from your partner, your family, your workplace, or anywhere else. Learn how to recognize your exhaustion and reward yourself with the needed space and time to become whole again.

14. Consider counseling

Professional counseling can seem intimidating at first, especially if you aren't ready to accept that there's anything "really wrong" with you.

But counseling can help anyone, regardless of their issues or conditions. Having that professional space to talk to someone who will understand can improve your situation tremendously.

15. Rely on support

There are groups and organizations out there filled with individuals who are facing the same issues and problems as you.

Self-Care is never selfish

Breaking your personal cycle of codependency means forcing your mind from a general shift of caring for others to caring for yourself, and this requires believing in a single mantra: self-care is never selfish.

Your happiness and self-worth are just as important as your partner's, and until both you and your partner recognize and acknowledge that, you will never truly turn away from codependency.

The most important thing to remember is that codependency is a learned behavior, not a disorder you are born with, and this means it can be unlearned.

Accept your need for major steps towards self-growth, and start discovering true sources for your self-worth.

Conclusion

Being codependent is hard, and many of us will continue to deny that we are codependent. That's just one of the signs!

No matter where you are on your codependent journey, remember that being codependent isn't beneficial for you or the other person. You need mutually beneficial relationships that make both people happy.

In fact, many things can slowly infect a marriage — not just codependency. If not dealt with correctly, these problems can metamorphosize into infidelity and disconnectedness.